Scottish Slimmers

simple

D0928399

contents

meat   4

fish   12

poultry   20

Key to recipes

meat

SERVES two | 175 **7** **8**

steak & tomato stacks

- spray oil
- ½ red onion, thinly sliced
- 115g/4 oz mushrooms, sliced
- salt and freshly ground black pepper
- 2 x 125g/4½ oz lean fillet steaks, all fat removed
- 1 beefsteak tomato, cut into 4 horizontal slices
- wild rocket leaves, to garnish
- oil-free vinaigrette for drizzling

1 Spray a frying pan lightly with oil and cook the red onion for about 5 minutes until softened.

2 Add the mushrooms and sauté for a further 5 minutes, until the mushrooms are golden and the onion is starting to caramelise. Season to taste with salt and black pepper.

3 Meanwhile, grill the fillet steaks on a hot, ridged grill pan until cooked on both sides, according to taste.

4 To assemble the stacks, place a tomato slice in the centre of a serving plate and place a cooked steak on top. Cover with another tomato slice and top with a little pile of mushrooms and red onion. Arrange a swirl of rocket on top and drizzle with vinaigrette. Repeat the process with the other stack and serve.

quick kebabs

- 250g/9oz lean mince
- ¼ tsp cumin
- ¼ tsp mixed spice
- ¼ tsp garlic powder
- ½ tsp paprika
- salt and pepper
- 4 rounded dspn low-fat natural yoghurt
- ½ tsp mint sauce
- 2 small 60g/2oz naan breads
- no-Check salad to serve

1 Pre-heat oven to 190°C/gas mark 5.

2 Mix spices into mince and season well with salt and pepper. Place mixture on a non-stick baking tray or roasting tin and flatten out to a rectangle approx. 10 x 15 cm/4 x 6 inches. Bake 15 minutes.

3 Remove tray from oven and drain surplus fat. Warm naan breads in the oven for a couple of minutes.

4 Meanwhile, transfer meat to a plate, cut in half, then cut each half into 5 or 6 strips. Stir the mint sauce into the yoghurt.

5 Serve each person with 1 naan bread topped with half the kebab pieces and yoghurt and accompany with no-Check salad.

SERVES **two** | 350 **14** **7**

steak, fresh tomato & basil pasta

- **200g/7 oz lean rump or frying steak**
- **1 tsp olive oil**
- **1 large clove garlic, crushed**
- **175g/6 oz fresh plum tomatoes, roughly chopped**
- **12 large basil leaves, torn**
- **salt and black pepper**
- **115g/4 oz pasta twirls**

1 Cook pasta in lightly salted boiling water until just tender.

2 Cut steak into small strips across the grain. Heat oil in a frying pan and sear steak quickly.

3 Add garlic and tomatoes and stir-fry 2-3 minutes. Season with salt and plenty of black pepper, add basil and cook 1 minute.

4 Drain pasta and serve half to each person topped with half the steak and tomatoes.

pork with red onion & balsamic vinegar

SERVES **two** | 200 **8** ⑥

- 250g/9 oz lean pork cubes
- 1 red onion, sliced
- spray oil
- 1 clove garlic, crushed
- 2 tbsp balsamic vinegar
- 200ml/7 fl.oz chicken stock

1 Spray a non-stick saucepan with oil and heat. Add the pork and onions and cook a few minutes until the pork is browned all over.

2 Add the garlic, balsamic vinegar and chicken stock and bring to a simmer.

3 Cover the pan and simmer gently for about 1 hour or until the pork is very tender. Stir occasionally.

pork, pepper & apricot brochettes

SERVES **two** | 250 **10** ⑥

- **4 bamboo skewers**
- **1 tbsp light soy sauce**
- **1 dspn runny honey**
- **1 dspn lemon juice**
- **250g/9 oz lean pork cubes**
- **12 ready-to-eat semi-dried apricots**
- **1 red or green pepper**

1 Soak the bamboo skewers in cold water at least 30 minutes to prevent scorching.

2 Mix together the soy sauce, honey and lemon juice in a shallow dish. Toss in the pork and apricots and leave to marinate at least 30 minutes.

3 Pre-heat the grill.

4 De-seed the pepper and cut into squares. Thread the skewers with alternating pieces of pork, apricot and squares of pepper.

5 Grill the brochettes, turning occasionally, until the pork is cooked through and peppers are charred at the edges.

fish

SERVES **two** | **4** **10** **16** **18**

salmon & lemon cream conchiglie

- **100g/3½ oz conchiglie (pasta shells)**
- **1 unwaxed lemon**
- **180-200g can skinless & boneless pink salmon**
- **142ml pot single cream**
- **salt and black pepper**

1 Cook pasta shells in lightly salted boiling water until just tender.

2 Grate the zest from the lemon and retain the lemon for squeezing.

3 Drain the salmon and put into a small saucepan together with the cream and lemon zest. Heat very gently, stirring now and again. Do not allow to boil.

4 Season the cream sauce with salt, black pepper and a good squeeze of lemon juice.

5 Drain pasta well and serve half to each person topped with half the sauce.

tuna pesto salad

SERVES two | 390 | 16 | 13

- 100g/3½ oz three-colour pasta twirls (or other shape)
- 150g/5 oz frozen minted peas
- 180-200g can tuna chunks in brine
- 2 tbsp green pesto
- 2 dspn freshly grated parmesan cheese

1 Cook pasta in lightly salted boiling water until just tender, adding frozen peas about 5 minutes before end of cooking time.

2 Drain tuna and lightly flake.

3 Drain pasta and peas and return to saucepan.

4 Add flaked tuna and fork through. Add pesto and mix gently. Cover and allow to warm through a few minutes.

5 Serve half the mixture to each person sprinkled with freshly grated parmesan cheese.

SERVES one | 300 12 2

cajun prawn skewers & rice

- **2 bamboo skewers**
- **1 small red onion**
- **1 small courgette**
- **1 small red pepper**
- **6 raw, peeled king or tiger prawns**
- **6 cubes pineapple**
- **spray oil**
- **60g/2 oz basmati rice**
- **salt**
- **½ tsp Schwartz Cajun Grill & Sizzle**
- **no-Check salad to serve**

1 Soak the bamboo skewers in water at least 30 minutes to prevent scorching.

2 Cut the onion into wedges, slice the courgette and cut the pepper into squares.

3 As the onions take longer to grill than the other vegetables, grill or microwave them for 2 or 3 minutes first.

4 Thread all the vegetables, pineapple and prawns alternately onto the skewers and spray with oil. Pre-heat the grill. Start to cook the rice in lightly salted water.

5 Grill the skewers under a medium-hot grill about 10 minutes, turning once. Sprinkle one side of the skewers with half the Cajun Grill & Sizzle and grill 1-2 minutes. Turn over and repeat.

6 Serve skewers with cooked rice accompanied by no-Check salad.

SERVES four | 200 | 8 | 3

haddock & cider casserole

- **700g/1½ lb haddock, skinned**
- **4 tomatoes, skinned and sliced**
- **115g/4 oz mushrooms, sliced**
- **1 tbsp chopped parsley or chives**
- **salt and black pepper**
- **150 ml/5 fl.oz dry cider or dry white wine**
- **2 tbsp fresh white breadcrumbs**
- **30g/1 oz Edam cheese, grated**

1 Pre-heat oven to 180°C/gas mark 4.

2 Wash the fish, cut into 5 cm/2 inch cubes and put in an ovenproof dish.

3 Cover with tomatoes, mushrooms, parsley or chives and seasoning.

4 Pour over cider or wine. Cover with foil and cook in the oven 20-25 minutes.

5 Sprinkle with breadcrumbs and cheese and brown in oven or under the grill.

kedgeree with a difference

juice of 1 large lemon
2 tbsp runny honey
2 dspn soy sauce
1 tsp grated fresh ginger or good pinch ground ginger
225g/8 oz haddock fillet, cubed
85g/3 oz prawns
85g/3 oz basmati rice
½ Knorr Pilau Rice cube, or chicken cube
spray oil
85g/3 oz frozen mixed sliced peppers
1 medium onion, chopped
1 clove garlic, crushed
1 medium banana, peeled and sliced
salt and pepper
chopped basil and chives to garnish (optional)

1 Mix together the lemon juice, honey, soy sauce and ginger to make a marinade. Add the haddock and prawns and leave for at least 30 minutes.

2 Boil the rice with the ½ stock cube. Drain off any excess liquid.

3 Spray pan or wok with oil and fry the peppers and onions for 3-4 minutes. Add the garlic, haddock and prawns with the marinade and stir-fry a further 3 minutes.

4 Add cooked rice, banana slices and season to taste. Stir-fry 2 minutes more. Serve sprinkled with chopped basil and chives.

poultry

SERVES **two** | 275 **11** **7**

turkey rolls

2 x 125g/4½ oz turkey escalopes
30g/1 oz lean, trimmed proscuitto (eg. Parma or
Serrano ham)
grated zest of ½ an unwaxed lemon
1 tbsp finely grated parmesan cheese
1 tbsp finely chopped fresh parsley
salt and black pepper
1 tsp olive oil
60g/2 oz button mushrooms, sliced
100 ml/3½ fl.oz Marsala or sweet sherry
1 tbsp half-fat crème fraîche
chopped parsley to garnish

1 Place the escalopes between 2 sheets of cling film
and beat out with a rolling pin until thin.

2 Chop the proscuitto and mix with the lemon zest,
parmesan, chopped parsley and a little seasoning.

3 Scatter the mixture over the escalopes, roll up tightly
and secure with wooden cocktail sticks.

4 Heat the oil in a frying pan and cook the turkey
rolls and mushrooms until browned all over. Add the
Marsala or sherry and let it bubble away gently for 10
minutes until reduced and the turkey is cooked.

5 Stir in the crème fraîche and serve sprinkled
with chopped parsley. Steamed green no-Check
vegetables make a good accompaniment.

chicken with pesto pasta

SERVES **two** 400 16 9

2 x 125g/4½ oz skinless chicken breasts
spray oil
1 red pepper, de-seeded and sliced
1 yellow pepper, de-seeded and sliced
2 cloves garlic, crushed
115g/4 oz wholewheat pasta twirls
1 tbsp green pesto
salt and black pepper
basil leaves to garnish

1 Cut the chicken into thin strips. Stir-fry briskly over high heat in a frying pan sprayed with oil until the chicken is golden and cooked through. Remove and set aside.

2 Cook pasta in a large saucepan of lightly salted boiling water until just tender.

3 Meanwhile, add the peppers and garlic to the frying pan and cook about 10 minutes until tender, stirring occasionally. Return chicken to the pan and warm through.

4 Drain the pasta well and stir in the pesto until it is lightly coated. Tip the pasta into the chicken and peppers, season to taste and serve garnished with torn basil leaves.

SERVES two | 200 | 8 | 5

stir-fried lemon chicken

250g/9 oz skinless chicken breasts, cut into strips
½ tsp sesame oil
½ tsp sesame seeds
juice of 1 lemon
1 tbsp sweet chilli sauce
1 tbsp soy sauce
spray oil
115g/4 oz small broccoli florets
115g/4 oz sugar snap peas, trimmed
4 spring onions, sliced diagonally
2 garlic cloves, crushed
2.5 cm/1 inch piece fresh ginger, peeled and chopped
1 small red chilli, de-seeded and chopped
2 tbsp hot water

1 Put the strips of chicken in a bowl with the sesame oil and seeds. Stir well to coat lightly.

2 Mix the lemon juice, sweet chilli sauce and soy sauce in a small bowl and set aside.

3 Heat a wok or deep pan and stir-fry the chicken 4-5 minutes until cooked through and golden. Remove and keep warm.

4 Spray pan with oil and tip in the broccoli, sugar snaps, spring onions, garlic, ginger and chilli. Stir-fry 2-3 minutes then stir in the lemon sauce and hot water. Cover the pan and cook 2-3 minutes until broccoli and sugar snaps are just tender.

5 Add the cooked chicken and heat through about 1 minute.

SERVES **one** | **375** **15** **10**

ten minute tandoori

- a few lettuce leaves
- 1-2 spring onions, sliced
- lemon juice
- black pepper
- 1 tomato sliced
- ½ tsp mint sauce
- 1 medium skinless chicken breast
- 1 level dspn Patak's Tandoori Curry Paste
- 1 mini naan bread

1 Arrange lettuce and spring onions on a serving plate, season with black pepper and lemon juice to taste. Arrange sliced tomato and dot with mint sauce.

2 Cut the chicken breast into about 10 cubes. Put the curry paste into a cold non-stick pan. Stir in the chicken to coat.

3 Turn heat to high and cook 4-5 minutes, stirring continuously, until starting to colour and char slightly. Turn down heat to medium, add 1 tbsp water and continue stirring and "scraping" about 3-4 minutes until water has evaporated and chicken is cooked through.

4 Warm naan bread in oven or toaster and serve together with the salad and warm cooked chicken.

wild chicken salad

- **30g/1 oz raw weight or 75g/2½ oz cooked weight white and wild rice**
- **60g/2 oz cooked chicken, finely chopped**
- **1 tbsp low-calorie mayonnaise**
- **7g/¼ oz cashew nuts**
- **8 cubes pineapple**
- **salad leaves**
- **8 seedless green grapes**

1 If not already cooked, boil rice and allow to cool completely.

2 Gently stir chicken into the rice with the mayonnaise until mixed and coated.

3 Fold in the cashew nuts and pineapple.

4 Serve on salad leaves garnished with green grapes.

Tip: If making for a special occasion serving more people, increase quantities accordingly and use fresh pineapple. Cut pineapple in half keeping shells in tact so that mixture can be served in the pineapple shells.

meat
free

SERVES | two | 215 9 5

cauliflower & broccoli gratin

- 1 small cauliflower, divided into florets
- 1 small head broccoli, divided into florets
- 2 level tbsp cornflour
- 300 ml/10 fl.oz skimmed milk
- 125g/4½ oz fat-free natural fromage frais
- salt and black pepper
- ½ tsp Dijon mustard
- 60g/2 oz half-fat cheddar
- 4 cherry tomatoes, halved
- 2 tbsp fresh breadcrumbs

1 Cook the cauliflower and broccoli florets in a large pan of lightly salted boiling water until just tender. Drain well.

2 Blend the cornflour with a little of the cold skimmed milk. Pour the remaining milk into a saucepan and bring to the boil. Stir in the cornflour, reduce heat and simmer gently, stirring continously for about 2 minutes, until thickened.

3 Remove the pan from the heat and beat in the fromage frais, seasoning, mustard and three-quarters of the grated cheddar.

4 Arrange the cauliflower and broccoli with the cherry tomatoes in an ovenproof dish. Pour over the cheese sauce and sprinkle with the breadcrumbs and remaining grated cheddar.

5 Pop under a pre-heated hot grill for 4-5 minutes until bubbling and golden brown.

indian
summer pasta

SERVES **one** 380 15 7

1 medium courgette
2-3 broccoli florets
good handful of frozen sliced green beans
60g/2 oz farfalle (pasta bows) or other pasta shapes
1 dspn cornflour
125 ml/4½ fl.oz skimmed milk
30g/1 oz mature half-fat cheddar, grated
salt and black pepper
1 dspn grated parmesan cheese

1 Slice the courgette and cut the brocolli florets in half if large.

2 Cook all the vegetables and pasta in lightly salted boiling water until tender.

3 Mix the cornflour, milk and half-fat cheese together in a small saucepan. Bring to the boil, stirring continuously until thickened. Season to taste.

4 Drain the pasta and vegetables very well. Serve topped with the cheese sauce and grated parmesan cheese.

SERVES	350	14	⑪
two			

spicy bean-filled yorkshires

- 1 medium onion, chopped
- 1 green pepper, chopped or a good handful of frozen sliced mixed peppers
- spray oil
- 400-425g can kidney beans
- 400g can chopped tomatoes
- good pinch of cumin
- good pinch of garlic powder
- 1 Oxo vegetable cube
- 1 tsp chilli powder (or to taste)
- 4 Aunt Bessie's frozen 4-minute Large Yorkshire Puddings (not giant size!)
- green beans or other no-Check vegetables to serve

1 Soften the onion and peppers in a saucepan sprayed with oil, adding a little water now and again to prevent sticking.

2 Drain and rinse the kidney beans. Add the tomatoes, kidney beans, cumin, garlic powder, crumbled vegetable cube and chilli powder to the pan. Mix well and simmer gently 10-15 minutes to thicken sauce and allow flavours to develop.

3 Warm the Yorkshires according to instructions on the pack. Divide the spicy bean mixture between the 4 Yorkshires and serve two to each person accompanied by green beans or other no-Check vegetables.

SERVES **two** | 365 15 8

vegetable & rice loaf

- **300g/10 oz boiled rice (made from 115g/4 oz dry weight)**
- **225g/8 oz cooked and chopped no-Check vegetables, e.g. carrots, onions, mushrooms, leeks**
- **60g/2 oz mature half-fat cheddar, grated**
- **1 egg**
- **1 tsp curry powder**

1 Pre-heat oven to 150°C/gas mark 2.

2 Combine all the ingredients together in a bowl, mixing well. Grease a loaf tin, line with foil and pour in mixture.

3 Place loaf tin in another ovenproof dish and add water to come halfway up the outside of the loaf tin. Bake approximately 45 minutes, or until loaf has set.

4 Serve either hot or cold cut into slices.

hot as you like curry

SERVES | four | 200 8 8

- **2 onions, chopped**
- **spray oil**
- **4 level tbsp Patak's Curry Paste, Mild, Medium, Madras or Extra Hot**
- **450g/1 lb frozen vegetable mixture, e.g. broccoli, cauliflower, peas, carrots, sweetcorn, etc.**
- **2 x 400g cans chopped tomatoes**
- **300g/10 oz potato, peeled and cubed**
- **1 tbsp mango chutney**

1 Soften onions in a large saucepan sprayed with oil. Add curry paste and cook 1 minute, stirring continuously.

2 Add remaining ingredients to the pan and stir well.

3 Bring to the boil, then simmer approximately 20 minutes until the vegetables are tender.

cheese & eggs

 artichoke, bacon & emmental ciabatta

SERVES four | 350 **14** **⑬**

- **1 ciabatta loaf, approx. 300 g/10 oz**
- **400g can artichoke hearts in brine**
- **100g/3½ oz lean, trimmed back bacon**
- **4 dspn tomato purée**
- **100g/3½ oz emmental cheese, grated**
- **no-Check salad to serve**

1 Pre-heat oven to 190°C/gas mark 5.

2 Cut ciabatta horizontally across, then cut each half in two to make 4 bases. Drain artichokes and cut in quarters. Chop the bacon.

3 Spread 1 dspn tomato purée on the bread side of each base. Scatter with grated emmental and arrange artichoke hearts and chopped bacon on top.

4 Place ciabattas on a baking tray and bake approximately 10 minutes until the crust is crispy and bacon is cooked. Serve 1 ciabatta to each person accompanied by no-Check salad.

poached egg & pepperoni pasta

SERVES one | 400 16 12

- **60g/2 oz linguine or spaghetti**
- **Dash of vinegar**
- **1 large Lion Quality egg**
- **4 tbsp low-fat pasta sauce**
- **15g/½ oz pepperoni slices**
- **15g/½ oz rocket leaves**

1 Boil pasta in lightly salted boiling water until just tender.

2 Meanwhile, fill a non-stick pan with 2 cm/1 inch cold water and dash of vinegar. Bring to a gentle simmer, crack in egg and poach 3-4 minutes.

3 Drain pasta and stir in the pasta sauce, pepperoni and rocket, tossing well to mix.

4 Transfer to a serving bowl and top with the poached egg.

| SERVES one | 280 | 11 | 5 |

quick tricolore pasta

- **60g/2 oz quick cook macaroni**
- **114g/ 4 oz frozen spinach**
- **30g/1 oz mature half-fat cheddar**
- **3-4 cherry tomatoes, quartered**

1 Cook macaroni in lightly salted boiling water until just tender. Drain well.

2 Put spinach in a microwavable bowl. Cover and cook on high approximately 2 minutes or until completely defrosted and warmed through.

3 Cut cheese into small dice. Add macaroni, cheese and tomatoes to the spinach and mix well.

4 Cover and microwave on high about 1 minute more. Eat straight from the bowl!

potato nest

SERVES **one** **380** **15** **11**

- **1 large potato**
- **a little skimmed milk**
- **30g/1 oz mature half-fat cheddar, grated**
- **salt and pepper**
- **1 egg**

1 Pre-heat oven to 200°C/gas mark 6.

2 Peel and boil the potato. Mash with a little skimmed milk. Add half the grated cheese and season to taste.

3 Place potato in an ovenproof dish and make a well in the centre. Crack the egg into the well and sprinkle over the remaining grated cheese.

4 Bake approximately 20 minutes or until golden brown and egg is cooked.

sweet treats

| SERVES four | 140 | 6 | 5 |

lemon meringue flan

- **2 level tbsp cornflour**
- **175 ml/6 fl.oz water**
- **3 tbsp lemon juice**
- **7 tbsp heat-stable granulated sweetener (e.g. Splenda)**
- **2 medium eggs, yolks and whites separated**
- **85-100g fluted sponge flan case**

1 Pre-heat oven to 150°C/gas mark 2.

2 Place cornflour in a small saucepan. Mix to a smooth cream with a little of the water. Stir in remaining water. Bring to the boil, stirring continuously, then reduce heat and simmer 1 minute, continuing to stir thoroughly.

3 Remove pan from heat. Beat in the lemon juice, 3 tbsp of the sweetener and the egg yolks until smooth and creamy.

4 Whisk egg whites until very stiff, then gently whisk in remaining 4 tbsp sweetener.

5 Pour lemon mixture into the flan case. Pile egg whites over top of flan ensuring a good seal at the edges. Bake in oven 40-45 minutes until meringue is golden. Serve warm or cold.

crunchy topped summer fruits

SERVES | four | 200 | 8 | 4

- 3 tbsp granulated sweetener
- 250g/9 oz frozen mixed summer fruits, defrosted
- 275 ml/10 fl.oz skimmed milk
- 2 tbsp custard powder
- 250g/9 oz low-fat natural yoghurt
- few drops vanilla essence
- 60g/2 oz Jordans Crunchy Cereal
- 30g/1 oz raisins
- 1 tbsp sesame seeds

1 Stir 1 tbsp of the sweetener into the summer fruits, then divide equally between four glasses or serving dishes.

2 In a saucepan, mix the milk with the custard powder and bring to the boil, stirring continuously, until it has thickened. Stir in the remaining sweetener, natural yoghurt and vanilla essence.

3 Take the mixture off the heat, cover with a piece of greaseproof paper and leave to cool. When cool, pour over the fruit.

4 Mix the cereal with the raisins and sesame seeds and sprinkle over the custard to serve.

apple &
yoghurt layer

 SERVES **one** 150 6 0

1 large cooking apple
granulated sweetener to taste
125g small carton diet raspberry yoghurt
fresh raspberries to garnish (optional)

1 Peel, core and chop apple. Stew or microwave
with 1 tbsp water until soft. Sweeten with granulated
sweetener to taste and allow to cool.

2 Layer the cooked apple and the raspberry yoghurt in
a glass or serving dish, finishing with a layer of yoghurt.
Garnish with one or two fresh raspberries, if using.

irish nests

 SERVES **four** 195 8 5

4 level scoops vanilla ice cream
4 tbsp Bailey's Irish Cream
4 meringue nests
1 small can mandarin oranges in juice, drained
4 chocolate leaves to decorate

1 Put the ice cream in a bowl and allow to soften a few
minutes. Add the Bailey's and mix thoroughly with a
fork. Put the mixture into a piping bag and place in the
freezer to stiffen.

2 Place the meringue nests on 4 individual serving
plates. Arrange mandarin segments around the inside
of each nest.

3 Place a swirl of ice cream in the centre of each nest
taking care to cover the oranges. Decorate each
dessert with a chocolate leaf.

| SERVES | 95 | **4** | **0** |
| four | | | |

pear & raspberry surprise

- 4 large Williams pears
- water or diet lemonade for poaching
- 115g/4 oz fresh or frozen raspberries
- ½ sachet raspberry sugar-free jelly
- 150 ml/5 fl.oz boiling water
- 4 tbsp fat-free natural fromage frais
- 1 tbsp granulated sweetener, or to taste
- few drops vanilla essence

1 Peel the pears and from the bottom, carefully remove cores so that pears remain whole. Cut a slice from the bottom of each pear so they stand upright.

2 Gently poach the pears in water or diet lemonade until just tender, then leave to cool.

3 Dissolve the jelly crystals in the boiling water and allow to cool but not set.

4 Stuff the hole from where the core was removed with raspberries (no need to defrost if using frozen raspberries). Pour jelly through the raspberries and cool until set.

5 Mix the fromage frais with the sweetener and vanilla essence to taste and serve a spoonful with each pear.